# A vegetable timeline

**8000–5000 BC**

Potatoes are first grown in Peru.

**2680 BC**

Lettuce is cultivated in Egypt.

**1000 BC**

Cabbages and kale are grown by the Celts.

**100 BC**

Spinach is first cultivated in what is Iran today.

**3500 BC**

Onions, leeks and garlic are grown in Egypt.

**200 BC**

The Romans start to grow asparagus.

**2000 BC**

Egyptian temple paintings are created of a purple plant that may be a carrot.

**1853**

Crisps are
invented.

**c. 1570**

The potato arrives
in Europe, initially
in Spain.

**1994**

Broccolini – baby
broccoli – is
cultivated.

**1845–1849**

Potato blight causes
the Irish famine.

**2008**

Tear-free onions
are developed in
a laboratory.

**AD 1492**

Christopher Columbus
introduces onions
to the Americas.

**1950s**

Vacuum cooling
makes it easier to cool
and store lettuce.

# Where vegetables come from

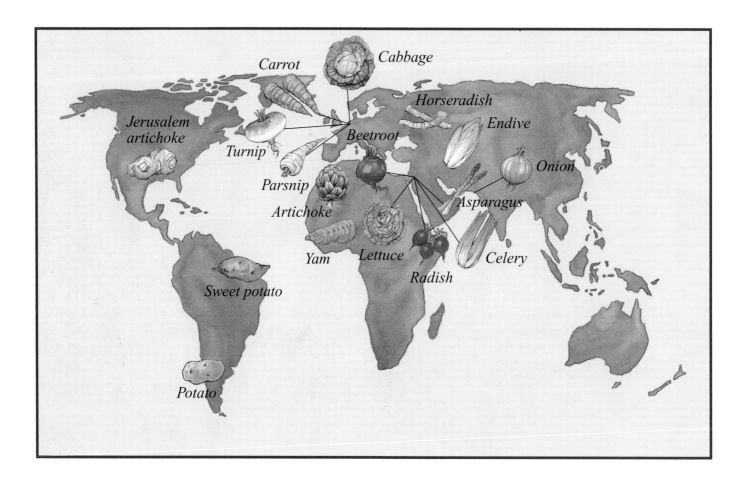

The above map shows the places where many of our most popular vegetables were first cultivated. As can be seen, many of them came from South America, the Middle East and northern Europe.

*Author:*

**Alex Woolf** studied history at Essex University, England. He is the author of over 60 books for children, many of them on historical topics. They include *1001 Hideous History Facts, You Wouldn't Want to be in the Trenches in World War I* and *You Wouldn't Want to Live Without Poo!*

*Artist:*

**David Antram** was born in Brighton, England, in 1958. He studied at Eastbourne College of Art and then worked in advertising for 15 years before becoming a full-time artist. He has illustrated many children's non-fiction books.

*Series creator:*

**David Salariya** was born in Dundee, Scotland. He has illustrated a wide range of books and has created and designed many new series for publishers in the UK and overseas. David established The Salariya Book Company in 1989. He lives in Brighton with his wife, illustrator Shirley Willis, and their son Jonathan.

*Editor:* **Jacqueline Ford**

*Editorial Assistant:* **Mark Williams**

Published in Great Britain in MMXVI by
Book House, an imprint of
**The Salariya Book Company Ltd**
25 Marlborough Place, Brighton BN1 1UB
www.salariya.com
www.book-house.co.uk

ISBN: 978-1-910706-40-4

# S A L A R I Y A

1 3 5 7 9 8 6 4 2

A CIP catalogue record for this book is available from the British Library.

Printed and bound in China.

Visit our website at **www.book-house.co.uk**
or go to **www.salariya.com** for **free** electronic versions of:
**You Wouldn't Want to be an Egyptian Mummy!**
**You Wouldn't Want to be a Roman Gladiator!**
**You Wouldn't Want to be a Polar Explorer!**
**You Wouldn't Want to sail on a 19th-Century Whaling Ship!**

PAPER FROM
SUSTAINABLE
FORESTS

# You Wouldn't Want to Live Without™
# Vegetables!

Written by
## Alex Woolf

Illustrated by
## David Antram

Series created by
## David Salariya

BOOK HOUSE
*a* SALARIYA *imprint*

# Contents

# Introduction

When someone mentions spinach, broccoli or kale, do you think YUCK? Is the cabbage still there on your plate at the end of a meal? What *are* these foods that our parents are so determined to make us eat? Why do we need them, and what would the world be like without them? Much better, right? Wrong! We'd be a lot unhealthier. Vegetables provide us with essential vitamins and minerals, which strengthen our bodies and stop us from getting sick. If served in imaginative ways – in a tasty sauce, for example, or roasted with a bit of olive oil, they can actually be quite delicious. Vegetables aren't just for eating either. They're also used to make things like dyes, lotions and adhesives. So next time you grumble about eating your greens, remember – you really wouldn't want to live without vegetables.

# What is a vegetable?

This is actually quite a hard question to answer. If you think you know your onions, here's a test for you. Which of the following foods are vegetables: aubergines, avocados, courgettes, cucumbers, peapods, pumpkins, tomatoes? The answer is none of them are! They're all fruits. It's confusing because in everyday language we call these foods vegetables, yet the strict definition of a vegetable is a seedless, edible part of a plant. All the above foods have seeds, which is why they're fruits. Carrots, onions, cabbages and potatoes are among the foods that are true vegetables.

TOMATO IN COURT. In 1883, the US Supreme Court ruled that a tomato was a vegetable, not a fruit, because it was eaten as a main course, not as dessert.

THE MUSHROOM is neither a fruit nor a vegetable – it's a fungus, which isn't even a member of the plant kingdom.

VEGETABLE PARTS. Most plants have roots, a stem, leaves, flowers and fruits. The vegetables we eat can be any of the first four of these.

FLOWER attracts pollinators such as birds and insects.

*Broccoli*

LEAF collects energy for the plant from sunlight.

*Lettuce*

STEM supports the weight of the plant.

*Celery*

ROOT anchors the plant to the ground.

*Carrots*

## You can do it!

Can you work out whether the following are fruits or vegetables? Celery, corn, peppers, radishes, spinach, squashes, rhubarb.

Answer: v, f, f, v, v, f, v

Eat your greens!

SEAWEED, popular in many coastal communities, is an algae, not a plant, so it's not a vegetable. But the 'crispy seaweed' often served in Chinese restaurants *is* a vegetable, because it's actually dried, deep-fried cabbage!

# How did we grow vegetables in the past?

**H**umans originally lived as hunter-gatherers. They hunted animals and ate wild plants. They would try eating the fruit, stems, leaves, flowers and roots of plants they encountered. Many must have been tried and then discarded because they tasted bad or made people sick. But a few plants proved to be tasty and safe, and these were encouraged to grow in forest clearings. This was how vegetable farming began, between 10,000 and 7000 BC.

**How do you do it, Heracles?**

THE ANCIENT GREEKS served veggies as a side dish known as *opson* (relish). A favourite food of the mighty hero Heracles was neither a vegetable nor a fruit. It was mashed beans, which are actually legumes (plant seeds that grow in long pods) but are often thought of as vegetables.

**I owe it all to mashed beans!**

For thousands of years, vegetable farming has followed an annual cycle of preparing the soil, sowing the seeds, tending the crops, and harvesting.

**He's faster than boiled asparagus!**

**It tastes better cooked.**

**Eat a cabbage leaf, and it will grow another. But dig up a potato, and the whole plant dies.**

THE EMPEROR AUGUSTUS had a fondness for asparagus, which he preferred lightly boiled. It inspired his favourite phrase, which he used to describe something fast…

THE ROMAN INVADERS introduced many vegetables to Britain, including garlic, onions, shallots, leeks, cabbages, celery, turnips and radishes. Leeks were so popular that they later became the national emblem of Wales.

VEGETARIANISM. Many Hindus, Buddhists and Jains are vegetarians because they don't believe in killing animals for meat. Jains try not to kill any plants either, so they avoid eating root vegetables.

# Do vegetables make us healthy?

Vegetables are an important part of a healthy diet. They are mostly low in fat and contain essential vitamins and minerals. They also supply us with dietary fibre, helping digestion. People who regularly eat vegetables are less likely to suffer from cancer, strokes and cardiovascular disease (disease of the heart or blood vessels). Most doctors recommend between five and nine servings of fruit and vegetables daily for a healthy diet.

## A balanced diet

*Can this be one of my five-a-day?*

*Protein*

*Vitamins, minerals and fibre*

*Fats and oils*

*Carbohydrates*

A BALANCED DIET contains all the nutrients you need to stay healthy and active. The main groups of nutrients are proteins; carbohydrates; fats and oils; and vitamins, minerals and fibre.

SCURVY, a disease caused by a lack of vitamin C, was once a big problem on sea voyages. In 1768, Captain James Cook discovered that adding vegetables to sailors' diets helped prevent scurvy.

No.

**You can do it!**

1. Keep vegetables where you can see them, so you're more likely to eat them.
2. Try out new veggies. Variety is healthy.
3. Skip the potatoes and instead eat veggies more packed with vitamins and minerals.

Something in this makes people healthy - but what?

MINERALS. Calcium (broccoli, celery, spring onion) fortifies bones and teeth; iron (spinach, Swiss chard, leeks) helps red blood cells; and potassium (all vegetables) helps muscles and nerves, and may prevent high blood pressure.

TOXINS. Some vegetables contain toxins (poisonous substances), which ward off insects and predators that might attack the plant. These can cause stomach ailments if eaten raw, but cooking should destroy any toxins.

DISCOVERY. In the early 1900s, scientists realised that foods such as vegetables provided certain essential nutrients that the body couldn't make by itself. These were called vitamins.

VITAMINS. Vitamin A (carrots, spinach, broccoli) stimulates new cell growth; vitamin B (green vegetables) converts food into energy; and vitamin C (sprouts, cabbage, cauliflower) strengthens the immune system.

11

# What are the origins of the onion?

Onions have been adding flavour to meals all over the world for thousands of years. The ancient Egyptians worshipped the onion. They saw it as a symbol of eternity because of its round shape and multiple layers. Onions have been used in many folk remedies. Whatever their medicinal value, they're certainly healthy, being rich in vitamin C and a good source of fibre. They can be eaten raw or cooked. They belong to the *Allium* family, which also includes garlic, chives, shallots and leeks.

*Place this under your pillow and it will help you sleep.*

*I swear those onions are looking at me!*

*It will make me run faster!*

ONION EYES. Ancient Egyptians buried onions with the pharaohs, and even placed them in the mummies' eye sockets!

ATHLETE'S FRIEND. Ancient Greek athletes drank onion juice and rubbed onions on their bodies before competing in the Olympic Games.

## How it works

Onions make you cry when you chop them because they contain chemicals called sulphur compounds. These form into a gas when the onion is chopped, and this irritates the eyes, causing them to tear up.

*Just what we always wanted!*

*Scalpel... Forceps...Onion...*

IN MEDIEVAL TIMES, onions were not only eaten, but also used to treat headaches, snakebites and hair loss. They were valued highly enough to be accepted as a rent payment or even as a wedding gift.

THE ROMANS ate onions regularly, and also used them as a remedy for poor vision, dog bites, mouth sores, toothaches, dysentery and back pain.

IN COLONIAL AMERICA, Native Americans ate onions both raw and cooked. They used them to make dyes or poultices and their children even played with them as toys.

13

"French-style potatoes, Mr. President."

"Actually, they're Belgian…"

# Why are we passionate about potatoes?

Potatoes are among the most popular food crops in the world – yet 500 years ago, potatoes were unheard of outside of Peru in South America. The Incas of Peru began growing potatoes between 8000 and 5000 BC, but it wasn't until AD1532, when Spanish conquistadors reached Peru, that Europeans encountered the crop. By the 1570s, Basque sailors were growing them along the coast of northern Spain. Potatoes arrived in the American colonies in 1621. Before long, they had become a staple crop throughout Europe and the New World.

FRENCH FRIES. President Thomas Jefferson introduced fries to the US when he had 'potatoes served in the French manner' at an 1802 White House dinner. The Belgians claim that they are the real inventors of this dish.

POTATO FAMINE. Potato blight swept across Europe in the 1840s, ruining the crops. The Irish suffered the most. Almost a million people died. Another two million left Ireland, mostly for North America.

"Hey, these are great!"

CRISPS. In 1853, tycoon Cornelius Vanderbilt complained that his potatoes were cut too thick. The angry chef sliced some paper thin. Vanderbilt loved them, and crisps have been popular ever since.

POTATOES IN SPACE! In October 1995, potatoes became the first vegetable to be grown in space. One day, they may be used to feed astronauts on long space voyages to Mars and beyond.

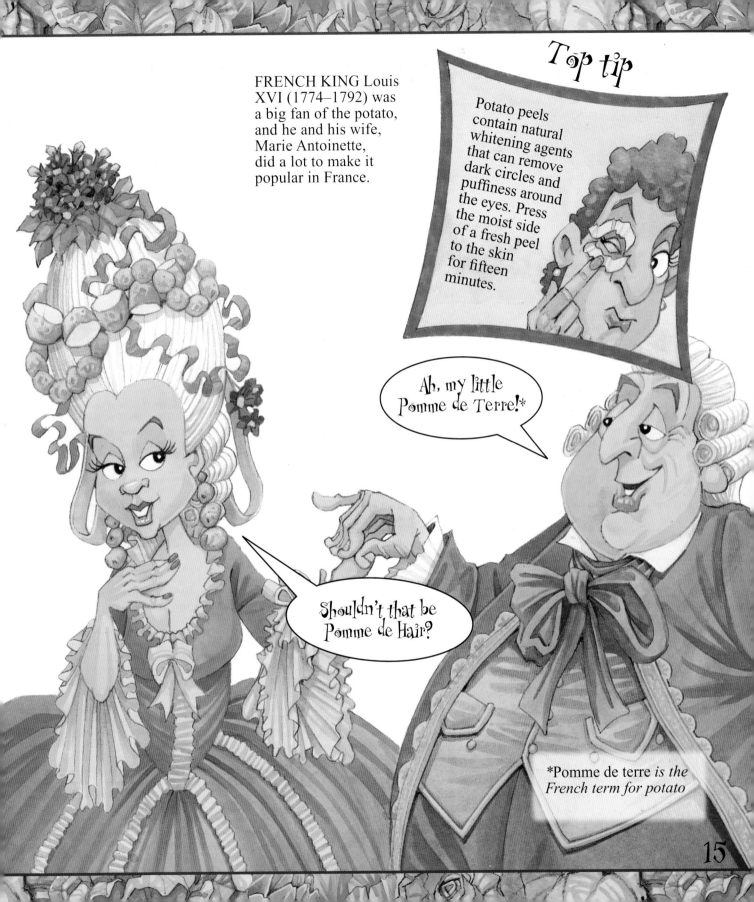

FRENCH KING Louis XVI (1774–1792) was a big fan of the potato, and he and his wife, Marie Antoinette, did a lot to make it popular in France.

**Top tip**

Potato peels contain natural whitening agents that can remove dark circles and puffiness around the eyes. Press the moist side of a fresh peel to the skin for fifteen minutes.

Ah, my little Pomme de Terre!*

Shouldn't that be Pomme de Hair?

*Pomme de terre *is the French term for potato*

15

# When did we get crazy about carrots?

The sweet, juicy, plump, orange carrot that we know and love today is a fairly recent vegetable, dating back only to the 16th century. Before that, carrots were purple, white or yellow. They were thin, small, usually forked, and had quite a bitter taste. Temple paintings in Egypt from 2000 BC show a purple plant that may have been a carrot. The Greeks and Romans grew carrot plants, though only for their seeds and leaves, which they used in their medicines. The Afghans were the first to grow carrot roots for food, in 3000 BC. The idea of carrots as food reached Asia Minor and Europe between the 8th and 9th centuries. Finally, Dutch growers got to work creating the modern orange carrot.

POISON ANTIDOTE. King Mithradates VI of Pontius (c.100 BC) used carrot seeds in a recipe for counteracting poisons – and it worked!

Carrots are orange because they contain a pigment called beta-carotene, which is also found in pumpkins, apricots and nectarines.

*Nice colour!*

HOUSE OF ORANGE. There is a legend that the Dutch bred the orange carrot to honour King William I of the royal House of Orange, but it's probably not a true story.

*How are they shooting down our bombers?*

*Carrots, sir!*

WORLD WAR II. British night fighter pilots used onboard radar to shoot down German planes. To keep the technology secret, a myth was spread that the pilots ate carrots to see better in the dark. This is still believed by many today.

*It's the future!*

THE BETA SWEET. Is the carrot changing? A group of scientists at Texas A&M University have developed a highly nutritious carrot with purple skin and orange flesh, containing cancer-preventing substances.

# What's the low-down on lettuce?

You're supposed to eat the stem!

**L**ettuce is the most popular of the salad vegetables and has been grown since ancient Egyptian times. But the lettuce of those days was a very different crop, with a long stem that was eaten like celery. Over the centuries, the Egyptians bred lettuce with broader, edible leaves. This type was known as romaine. Later, other forms of lettuce appeared, including butterhead (small, with soft, oily leaves) and iceberg (with a large, firm head).

MILKY PLANT. The name 'lettuce' comes from the Latin *lactis*, meaning milk, because of the milky sap, called latex, found in the stems and branches of lettuce plants.

SLEEPY SALAD. The ancient Romans believed that lettuce made people sleepy, so Emperor Domitian served it at the start of his feasts. He wanted to torment his guests by forcing them to stay awake in his presence.

Wake up!

Lettuce sleep...

Hmm...The leaves aren't bad.

**Top tip**

Lettuce is one of the few vegetables that you have to eat fresh. You can't freeze, can, dry or pickle it. The best place to store lettuce is in the crisper drawer of your refrigerator.

This is all we have.

Okay, let's put it together and see what we get.

CAESAR SALAD. In 1924, restaurateur Caesar Cardini invented a new salad using romaine lettuce, croutons and Parmesan cheese. Caesar salad became popular and renewed people's interest in lettuce.

ICEBERG. In the 1930s, to keep lettuce fresh during transportation across the US, it was covered with ice. As the train pulled into each stop, people would call out: 'The icebergs are coming!' That's how iceberg lettuce got its name.

19

# Why are we captivated by cabbage?

Ugh! Boiled cabbage! There must be poor people around.

abbage, from the French *caboche,* meaning 'head', has been grown for thousands of years. Loved by the ancient Greeks and Romans, it was spread throughout northern Europe by the conquering armies of Julius Caesar. Not only did they use cabbage for food, they also covered wounds with its leaves to reduce swelling. The popularity of cabbage spread among the peasantry during the Middle Ages, because it was so easy to grow.

DIOGENES, the Greek philosopher, advised a wealthy courtier: 'If you lived on cabbage, you would not need to flatter the powerful.' The courtier saw things the other way around.

If you flattered the powerful, you wouldn't need to live on cabbage!

VILE VEGETABLE. The nobility were suspicious of cabbage, which was rumoured to cause the plague (it didn't). Many found the strong aroma of boiling cabbage offensive. Yet for the peasants it was a highly nutritious food, full of vitamin C, minerals and fibre.

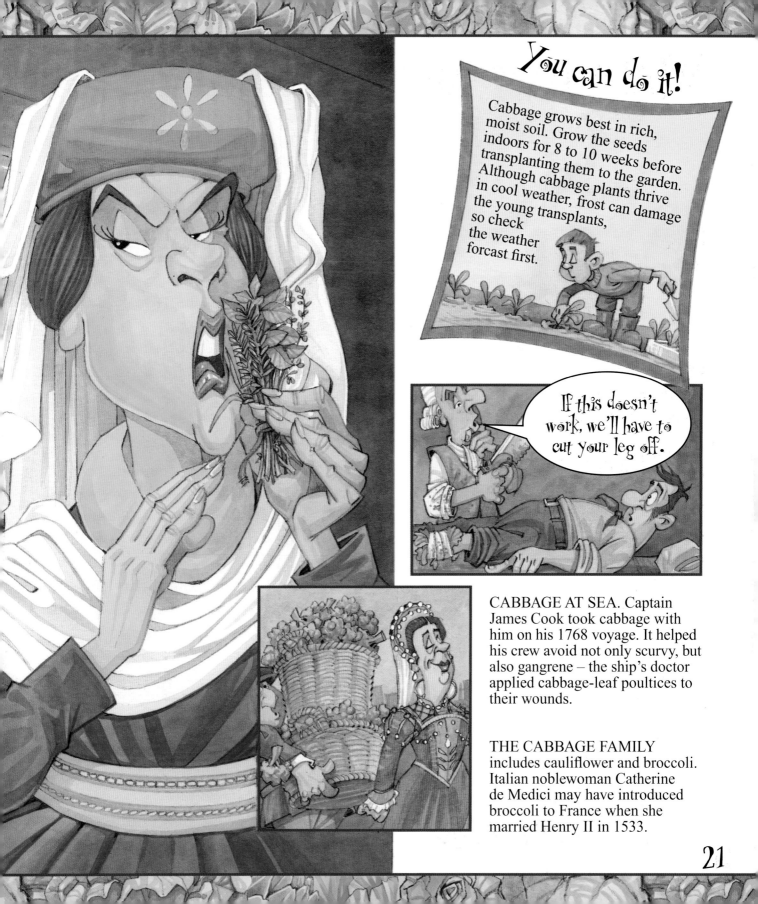

Cabbage grows best in rich, moist soil. Grow the seeds indoors for 8 to 10 weeks before transplanting them to the garden. Although cabbage plants thrive in cool weather, frost can damage the young transplants, so check the weather forcast first.

If this doesn't work, we'll have to cut your leg off.

**CABBAGE AT SEA.** Captain James Cook took cabbage with him on his 1768 voyage. It helped his crew avoid not only scurvy, but also gangrene – the ship's doctor applied cabbage-leaf poultices to their wounds.

**THE CABBAGE FAMILY** includes cauliflower and broccoli. Italian noblewoman Catherine de Medici may have introduced broccoli to France when she married Henry II in 1533.

21

# Are vegetables just for eating?

Vegetables are not just food. They are used in many other ways, both in factories and in homes. Potato starch, for example, is used in many different products, from packing material to glue. Lettuce sap has been used as a folk medicine for hundreds of years, treating people for coughs, anxiety, tension, pain and rheumatism (swollen, painful joints or muscles). You can rub an onion on insect bites or stings to ease the itchiness and pain. Vegetables can be a form of art, sculpted into imaginative shapes, from flowers to jack-o'-lanterns.

You smell like salad!

GOOD FOR THE SKIN. Lettuce can be used to relieve skin rashes. Today it is used as an ingredient in some soaps and skin lotions.

POLISHING METAL. Slice an onion and then crush it. Mix the crushed onion with water, then use a cloth to rub the mixture onto a metal surface. It will make cutlery gleam.

**You can't hurt me!**

## You can do it!

If you have a splinter that you can't remove, tape a piece of raw onion to it and leave it there for about an hour. The anti-inflammatory properties in the onion will draw the splinter to the skin's surface.

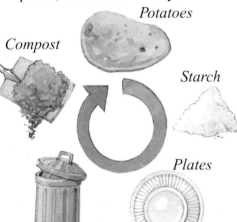

POTATO PLATES! Potato starch is frequently used as an eco-friendly, biodegradable form of plastic, used to make disposable plates, dishes and cutlery.

Potatoes

Compost

Starch

Plates

Bin

VEGETABLE DYES. Vegetables contain chemicals called polyphenols, which attach to fabric and dye it. That's why food can stain your clothes.

*ONIONS for yellow or brown dye*

*SPINACH for green dye*

*BEETROOT for red or pink dye*

VEGETABLE CARVING may have begun in ancient China or Japan. Today, carved vegetables are often used as a garnish when serving food. Carrots, radishes and shallots are great for carving.

# How are vegetables grown and preserved?

For thousands of years, vegetables were grown on small plots of land. They had to be eaten fresh, so any excess had to be sold quickly in nearby towns. The last two centuries have seen big advances in cultivation techniques. The use of better fertilisers, greenhouses, polytunnels and hydroponics have greatly increased yields, while advances in refrigeration technology have allowed growers to store their produce for longer. They can now grow large quantities of vegetables and sell them in bulk to towns and cities.

## From seed to stomach

*Plough the land*

*Sow the seeds*

*Water the plants*

*Harvest the vegetables*

*Sell the vegetables*

*Eat the vegetables*

Hydroponics is a way of growing vegetables without soil. They are grown indoors in water rich in mineral nutrients. The crops are better protected from weeds, weather, pests and diseases, but the yield is lower and more technical knowledge is needed.

GREENHOUSE. The glass traps the Sun's heat, keeping the greenhouse warm, so vegetables can be grown even in the winter.

RAISED-BED GARDENING. Vegetables are grown close together in raised beds enclosed by a frame. The soil is enriched with compost. The closeness of the plants prevents weed growth and conserves moisture.

Quick! Refrigerate it!

STORING. After a vegetable is harvested, it starts to lose moisture and vitamin C. Green leafy vegetables wilt quickly if not refrigerated. Root crops, like onions and potatoes, last longer.

At least my parsnips will be preserved.

PRESERVING. We can preserve vegetables by destroying germs or preventing their growth. This is often done by canning, freezing, pickling in vinegar, or boiling in sugar to create jams.

25

# Do vegetables affect the environment?

Eating vegetables doesn't only make us healthier, it also helps the planet. Vegetable farming uses up fewer natural resources than meat farming and causes less environmental damage. If we all ate less meat and more vegetables, it would reduce global warming: around 20 percent of all greenhouse gases, like methane, come from livestock farming. Eating less meat would also reduce the amount of land and water needed for farming, so fewer forests would need to be destroyed for cattle grazing.

WATER. It takes a whopping 6,992 litres of water to produce a pound (about half a kilogram) of beef. That includes the water needed to grow the grass and other food for the cow, plus water for drinking and cleaning. Compare that to vegetables, shown here.

*artichokes: 445 litres per pound*

*garlic: 323 litres per pound*

*lettuce: 127 litres per pound*

*asparagus: 977 litres per pound*

*broccoli: 155 litres per pound*

Why not try growing your own vegetables?
• It could save you money
• Gardening is a great form of exercise
• It will help you get your five daily portions of fruit and vegetables

MANY FARMERS use chemical pesticides and fertilisers on their crops. These contain nitrates, which leach into the ground and local waterways. Organic farmers avoid these chemicals.

This came from my garden.

LAND. A vegetarian family needs around 1 acre (0.4 hectare) of land to produce all the food it needs. The average, meat-eating modern family needs 20 acres (8 hectares). That's partly because most of our plant crops are consumed by livestock.

I've got a lot more land than you.

You need it.

FOOD MILES. Many supermarket vegetables are imported from distant countries on ships, planes and trucks, all of which pollute the atmosphere. That's why it's better to buy locally produced vegetables.

These come from the other side of the world.

# What happens to vegetables?

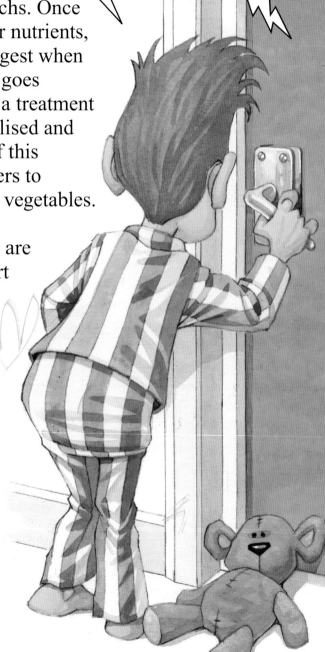

**What are you doing in there?**

**Playing my part in nature's cycle.**

**V**egetables end up in our stomachs. Once our bodies have absorbed their nutrients, we get rid of what we can't digest when we go to the toilet. Our waste goes through the sewage system to a treatment plant where it is cleaned, sterilised and then returned to the environment. Some of this sterilised waste, or sludge, is sold to farmers to fertilise soil. It may be used to grow more vegetables. So next time you don't want to eat your vegetables, remember how important they are for your health, and what an important part you play in helping them grow.

**It's disgusting!**

**It's natural.**

DECAY. Vegetables are living organisms, and they contain bacteria and fungi. These feed on the vegetables, causing them to spoil. Fungus appears as mould on the food's surface.

To reduce food waste, don't store broccoli, cauliflower or leafy greens next to apples, apricots, melons or figs. These fruits emit a gas called ethylene, which makes the vegetables decay faster.

FOOD POISONING. Microbes release chemicals that lower the vegetable's nutritional value. They may also release waste products that can make us sick, which is why we shouldn't eat vegetables that are going off.

If it's still firm, it's safe to eat after you've removed the sprouts.

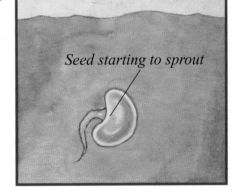

*Seed starting to sprout*

SPROUTED POTATOES. Potatoes are a thick part of the plant's root, called a tuber, and they contain buds. When exposed to light or warmth, the buds can grow into sprouts, or 'eyes'.

HUMUS. Many vegetables are thrown away uneaten, or never harvested. These decompose naturally, eaten by microbes in the earth to create a dark substance called humus that enriches the soil and makes it fertile.

# Glossary

**Bacteria**  A group of microorganisms, some of which can cause disease.

**Biodegradable**  Capable of being decomposed by bacteria or other organisms.

**Blight**  A plant disease, especially one caused by a fungus.

**Compost**  Decayed organic material used as plant fertiliser.

**Crisper drawer**  A drawer at the bottom of the fridge for storing vegetables.

**Cultivate**  To raise or grow crops in order to sell them.

**Dietary fibre**  Substances in food, such as cellulose and lignin, which help in the digestive process.

**Dysentery**  A disease of the intestines resulting in severe diarrhoea.

**Eco-friendly**  Not harmful to the environment.

**Emission**  The production and discharge of a gas.

**Fertiliser**  A substance added to soil to make it more fertile (capable of producing more crops).

**Fungus**  A family of organisms, including mushrooms, toadstools, moulds and yeasts, that feed on organic matter.

**Gangrene**  The death and decay of live tissues in a part of the body.

**Greenhouse gases**  Gases, such as carbon dioxide, that contribute to the greenhouse effect – the trapping of the sun's heat in the atmosphere.

**Immune system**  The organs and processes of the body that provide resistance to infection.

**Livestock**  Farm animals.

**Microbe**  A microorganism, such as a disease-causing bacterium.

**Mineral**  A solid, inorganic (not carbon-based) natural substance.

**Nitrates**  Chemicals used as fertiliser: sodium nitrate, potassium nitrate or ammonium nitrate.

**Nutrient**  A substance that provides nourishment essential for growth and a healthy life.

**Organic**  Relating to or obtained from living matter. Organic farming is farming without the use of chemical fertilisers or pesticides.

**Pesticide**  A substance used to destroy insects or other organisms that can be harmful to crops.

**Pickle**  To preserve fruit or vegetables using sugar, vinegar and brine.

**Pigment**  A substance in animal or plant tissue that gives it its colour.

**Pollinator**  Something that deposits pollen on a plant, allowing fertilisation.

**Polytunnel**  A long, polythene-covered frame under which seedlings or other plants are grown outdoors.

**Poultice**  A soft, moist material, often from a plant, applied to wounds to relieve soreness and inflammation.

**Radar**  A system for detecting the presence, direction, distance and speed of aircraft and other objects.

**Staple crop**  The main or most important crop.

**Starch**  A substance obtained from foods like potatoes and cereals that contains carbohydrates and is an important part of the human diet.

**Vitamin**  Any of a group of organic chemicals that are essential for growth and nutrition.

**Yield**  The amount of something, such as crops, that are produced.

# Index

# Top biggest vegetables

**Cabbage**: 62.71 kg
Grown by John Evans,
USA, 2012

**Sweet potato**: 37 kg
Grown by Manuel Pérez Pérez,
Spain, 2004

**Beetroot**: 23.4 kg
Grown by Ian Neale,
UK, 2001

**Broccoli**: 15.8 kg
Grown by John Evans,
USA, 1993

**Cauliflower**: 27.5 kg
Grown by Peter Glazebrook,
UK, 2014

**Carrot**: 9.1 kg
Grown by Peter Glazebrook,
UK, 2014

**Onion**: 8.5 kg
Grown by Tony Glover,
UK, 2014

**Potato**: 4.9 kg
Grown by Peter Glazebrook,
UK, 2011

# Vegetable carving

No one knows for sure when or where the art of vegetable carving began. Some say it started in 7th-century China. Emperor Zhong Zong wanted to thank the gods for his victory over his enemies, so he asked his cooks to carve mythical animal shapes out of vegetables.

Many people believe this art form first started in Japan, where it is known as mukimono. In ancient Japan, food was served on rough, unglazed plates, and chefs tried to improve the presentation of their dishes by adding an artistically cut or folded salad leaf as a garnish. By the 16th century, the art of mukimono had become part of every chef's training.

According to yet another theory, vegetable carving started in 14th-century Thailand during the Loi Krathong festival when decorated rafts were paraded through the streets. Nang Noppamart, a servant to the king, decided to carve a flower and a bird from a vegetable for her raft. The king was so impressed, he decreed that from then on, every woman should learn this new art form.

Whatever its origins, vegetable carving flourishes to this day, and not just in Asia. Throughout the world, people are experimenting with carving carrots, radishes and shallots into exquisitely intricate and delicate shapes.

# Did you know?

- It is actually possible to turn your skin a shade of orange by eating too many orange carrots.

- For the Incas, a unit of time was based on how long it took to cook a potato.

- Coleslaw, the cabbage-based salad, is based on the Danish words *kool*, meaning 'cabbage', and *sla*, meaning 'salad'.

- Drusus (13 BC–AD 23), son of Roman Emperor Tiberius, loved broccoli so much that he gorged himself on it, eating nothing else for an entire month. His urine turned bright green.

- Fossil pollen dating from the Eocene period (56–34 million years ago) has been identified as belonging to the carrot family.

- Although most scholars believe the modern orange carrot wasn't developed until the 17th century, there is an illustration of one in a Byzantine book dated AD 512. Maybe there was an earlier version of the orange carrot?

- Potatoes are a member of the nightshade family, which includes the poisonous belladonna plant.

- Most people know that New York's nickname is The Big Apple. Fewer people know that Chicago's name comes from the French version of a Native American word that means 'Stinky Onion.'

- According to country folklore, the thicker an onion's skin, the more severe the coming winter is likely to be.